A Taste
of the
Forest of Dean

A Taste
of the
Forest of Dean

A Forester's Family Menu
of Yesteryear

JENNY CARE

Best wishes
Jenny Care

THE CHOIR PRESS

First published in the United Kingdom in 2019 by
The Choir Press

ISBN 978-1-78963-060-2

A TASTE OF THE FOREST OF DEAN

A Foresters Family menu from yesteryear

———◄०►———

Gloucestershire is a unique county: split in two by the wild River Severn. To the west is the hilly, former industrial area of the Royal Forest of Dean and to the east is the rolling, green agricultural beauty of the quintessentially English idyll of the Cotswolds. Out of these two distinct regions, a food heritage has grown, flavoured by the differing landscapes, customs and history of the Gloucestershire people.

The Forest of Dean is a rough triangular plateau squeezed between the rivers Wye and Severn and topped by Herefordshire. Once upon a time, it was covered in woodland but gradually the timber was used for charcoal making and shipbuilding, reducing the forest to only 42 square miles.

There is evidence the forest was occupied in the Mesolithic period, and there is definite remains from Roman occupation in around 50 AD when they came to abstract the natural resources of coal, iron ore and ochre.

From the medieval times, the core of the Forest was used by Anglo-Saxons and then Normans as a personal hunting ground for the monarchy and was kept well stocked with wild boar and deer. Some of the earliest records for the Forest relate to Cnut levying heavy penalties on illegal hunting, and Edward the Confessor is known to have hunted there. The woodland was designated within defined boundaries with its own rules and laws, established by William the Conqueror, overseen by its own court and administration. King John frequently visited for sport, using St Briavels Castle as his hunting lodge, which was also the administrative centre of the Forest. By the 17th century, the Speech House was the kings abode when visiting this Royal playground.

Habitation and cultivation by ordinary people was not allowed within the Royal Demesne, and so scattered villages grew around the edges with trespass and poaching punished heavily with harsh sentences such as imprisonment or emasculation and blinding if caught. Death sentences were also served on many peasants, who were only trying to feed their families.

Before travel was effortless and widespread, and before corner shops and supermarkets graced the high street, Forest families lived a hand to mouth existence and relied on local produce that they could either grow, forage, rear, catch or poach, to provide nutritional, basic meals. Ordinary Foresters tended to live in simple stone cottages, with a pig sty attached and fairly large gardens for cultivating vegetables and fruit and for keeping poultry. A small herd of sheep may have been shepherded in the woods, along with the pigs, as part of the Commoners' Privileges. A few lucky residents might have afforded a cow. This enabled them to be fairly self-sufficient. Some of the recipes they devised still exist to this day, but most use ingredients that are difficult to acquire, or that seem rather unhealthy to a twenty-first century palette. What one must remember is that most Forest communities lived on a meagre wage scratched from the land or underground when employment was available, and that most housewives had to feed large families on these limited budgets.

In this book, I am going to set out a Forest of Dean menu that includes dishes of yesteryear that, with the odd exception, can be tried today. The recipes have been gleaned from old books, many owned by generations of Foresters who remember their mothers presenting such dishes at mealtimes when they were children. Many of the recipes reflect the limited cookery techniques that were available, like cooking over open fires, on a skillet, or in a large pot, where temperatures could not be easily regulated. I will make reference to the history behind some of the dishes and the ingredients used. In no way is it a definitive menu, but hopefully it will give you a flavour and a taste of this part of Gloucestershire and its more unusual dishes to tantalize your taste buds, or not!

Please note the recipes are in the authentic British imperial units and some are without oven temperatures, probably because open fires had no temperature gauges. There are conversion tables at the back.

MENU

A NOURISHING BOWL

—◦—

CATCH OF THE DAY

—◦—

DINNER IS SERVED

———◦———

SAY CHEESE!

———◦———

SWEET TOOTH!

TIME FOR TEA!

CHEERS!

———◀◦▶———

A NOURISHING BOWL

———◦———

Let us begin our gastronomic journey with the soup course. The amazing thing I discovered when researching this part of the menu was that milk was used a lot – milk from the local Gloucestershire cattle. Water may have been avoided because of the risk of contamination. In the Forest of Dean many cottages were without running water until the 1950s so water had to be carried from rivers or wells in heavy buckets and with no main sewers either, rivers and streams would not have been very clean, neither would well water have been very desirable, as it was of course untreated. Most country folk kept a cow or knew someone who did, so milk would have been an ideal substitute and a nutritious one at that.

WHITE FOAM SOUP was a traditional light and tasty soup made from staples found in even the poorest larder and often flavoured with celery, onions and mace. The recipe makes enough for six.

1 Onion, stick of Celery, clove of Garlic	1oz plain flour
2oz Butter	2 pints Milk
Small blade of Mace	1 tablespoon chopped parsley
2 eggs, separated. Yolks beaten	2oz double Gloucester cheese, grated
Salt and pepper to taste	

Finely dice the onion and celery and crush the garlic. In a saucepan melt the butter and stir in flour. Cook for a minute then gradually stir in milk stirring all the time. Bring to the boil, reduce heat and simmer for 2 minutes stirring continually. Add the celery, onion and mace and simmer until well flavoured. Remove from heat and cool slightly then stir in beaten egg yolks. Slowly reheat soup but <u>do not</u> allow to boil or you will end up with scrambled eggs! Season to taste and add grated cheese. Whisk egg whites until they form a stiff froth and carefully fold half into the soup using a large metal spoon. Place the other half into a soup tureen and carefully pour the soup over it. Sprinkle with chopped parsley. Serve immediately.

BRUSSEL SPROUT SOUP is thought to have evolved from a soup developed by the Romans who brought to Britain a small cabbage-like brassica, perhaps the forerunner of the Brussel sprout. In Rome, cabbage was considered a luxury and many regarded it as better than all other vegetables. They also used it for medicinal purposes such as relief from gout, headaches and the symptoms of poisonous mushroom ingestion. Pliny the Elder wrote about seven known variants of cabbage during his time, which included Pompeii, Cumae, and Sabellian cabbage. Except for nourishment, Ancient Egyptians and Romans ate larger amounts of cabbage before a night of drinking which allowed them to drink more.

By the thirteenth century, sprouts were widely cultivated, especially in Belgium, which is where they were named, and it was not long before many gardens in the Forest displayed rows of the vegetable, standing like soldiers ready in the cold winter months to produce a nourishing, nutritious soup! Possibly too much of this soup led to their downward slide in the popularity stakes!

1½ lbs Brussel sprouts, sliced

1 Carrot, Turnip, Onion, Celery stick

2 pints Milk 1oz butter

1oz Flour

2 Bay leaves and a bunch of Herbs

Salt, Pepper and a teaspoon of Sugar

Dice the carrot, turnip, onion, celery and with the Brussel sprouts boil in the milk, slightly seasoned with a little salt and sugar. Add the bay leaves and herbs and simmer for about 30 minutes. Remove the bay leaves

Love them or hate them – Brussel Sprouts – amazon.com.grocery

and pass all the vegetables through a sieve (or put in a blender). Save a few Brussels for a garnish. Add the pulp to the milk. Rub the butter and flour into a paste and whisk into the milk. Bring the soup to the boil and simmer for 2 minutes to cook out the flour. Season to taste and add a whole Brussel to each serving.

This is probably the only time over cooking the Brussels is acceptable! However, we all know overcooking vegetables removes all the nutrients and flavour so should you want to try this soup, reduce the simmering time by half and then put mixture in blender to produce a smooth soup.

CHESTNUT SOUP was another Roman introduction. Sweet Chestnut trees were planted in Britain by the Romans because they adored the fruit. The Forest of Dean area is very rich with Roman remains and there is a saying "Scratch Gloucestershire and find Rome"!!!

Chestnuts were foraged for free in the Forest and provided a filling meal. Before potatoes arrived in Britain in the sixteenth century, there was scarce access to wheat flour, so chestnuts were the main source of carbohydrates for Forest dwelling communities.

Sweet Chestnuts

1lb Sweet Chestnuts (Can of chestnut puree is acceptable if chestnuts out of season)

1 pint Milk	Chicken or Vegetable stock
4 tablespoons Cream	1 medium Potato diced
¼ teaspoon White Pepper	½ teaspoon Salt
½ teaspoon Sugar	Blade of Mace

Put chestnuts in a saucepan of unsalted water and boil for about 20 minutes until outer and inner skins peel off easily. Remove skins and put chestnuts in saucepan with milk and stock, potato, salt, pepper, mace and sugar. Bring to the boil and simmer for about 60 minutes until chestnuts are tender. Remove mace and discard. Blend chestnuts with a little of the liquid until a smooth puree is achieved. Return to the saucepan, add cream and bring to near boiling point stirring well. Check for seasoning. Serve at once.

POTATO SOUP or WHITE SOUP is another soup that uses milk and other staple larder ingredients and would have been a filling meal in itself for hungry, hardworking Foresters.

1 lb Potatoes diced	2 Onions or Leeks sliced
1½ pints milk	Stick of Celery diced
Blade of Mace	Lump of Sago

Boil all the ingredients together in 1 pint of the milk until they are cooked. Mix the sago in the rest of the milk. Blend the sago liquid into the soup and bring to the boil. Serve at once.

Sago (or tapioca) for many of us oldies is remembered as 'frog spawn' milk pudding. It is pure carbohydrate with very little protein, vitamins or minerals, but was often used as a 'tummy filler'. It was commonly used to thicken foodstuffs as an alternative to stale bread or potatoes. Cornflour can be used today.

Vintage Soup Tureen – very in keeping for Brussel Sprout Soup!
Picture from www.arket.com

CATCH OF THE DAY

—◄o►—

The Rivers Severn and Wye were good providers of fish for the dinner table and the unusual and sometimes dangerous methods of catching Salmon, Lampreys and Elvers made this a unique area in the history of fishing in Britain.

BAKED LAMPREYS or LAMPREY PIE are dishes rarely seen nowadays. The Lamprey has been around since before the dinosaurs and are a rare primitive parasitic eel-like fish, rather ugly but with a royal pedigree. The name

Lampreys - wikipedia

Lamprey comes from the Latin Lampreta, which means stone sucker or licker! The name refers to the fact that the fish use their mouths as suckers to adhere to other fish to gain sustenance. Locally they are called 'nine eyes' because along their sides they have 7 gills as well as their eye and nostril.

In medieval times, they were regarded as a delicacy. They are much meatier than normal fish due to their dense muscled physique and lack of bones. It is said leave a Lamprey out in the sun and its high fat content will melt away to nothing! It is practically boneless. They were very popular during religious fasting festivals as they could provide a more substantial meal than ordinary fish.

It is recorded that Henry I enjoyed Lampreys a little too much and succumbed to a 'surfeit of lampreys'. For all you 'Game of Thrones' aficionados you will know that 'Tyrion Lannister' is very fond of his Lamprey Pie cooked with wine, spices and covered in a crust!

Fishing for Lampreys is not for the faint hearted. In medieval times, they were caught by spears but over time, it was found easier to dig them out of the water! It was a case of wading into the river with a wooded shovel and digging into the bed of the watercourse and then throwing the contents onto

A Gloucestershire Royal Lamprey Pie – Gloucestershire Chronicle 11th June 1910

the bank. One then had to sift through the sand and stones to see if a Lamprey had been caught. It took some strength to lift a shovel full of sand, stone, water and hopefully Lampreys!

From the middle ages until 1836 it was customary for the Corporation of Gloucester to send a lamprey pie to the reigning monarch each Christmas. In the year 1200, the Gloucester Corporation officials forgot to send one to King John and were duly fined 40 marks (£250,000 in today's money) by the King for their neglect. Nowadays the monarch is sent a pie on special occasions only, such as a Coronation or Jubilee.

Recently in the Forest of Dean, action has been taken to help Lampreys migrate upstream to spawn. Blackpool Brook, which runs through Blakeney, has always been an important stream for migrating Lampreys and Eels, but the weir proved too difficult for the fish to get much further and so a by-pass has been built to ensure the protected fish can get to their spawning grounds. However, it does not mean that the fish will be available for the cook pot! They are critically endangered and protected!

The original ancient recipe would have seen the gutted fish baked slowly in a dish as below. Frying the fish tends to turn it into 'boot leather'!

2 scores of Lampreys

Butter, Salt & Pepper, Mace, Nutmeg, Cayenne Pepper

Tablespoon of water

To Serve: Vinegar, Mustard, and Sugar

Cut off the Lamprey heads behind the eyes. Layer them in a dish that has been greased with butter. Sprinkle with the seasonings mixed in the water. Repeat until the dish is full. Cover and cook in a slow oven for 2 hours. Leave to cool and serve with vinegar mustard and sugar. Alternatively, the fish can be cooked with a crust lid.

Personally, I think I'll give it a miss!

ELVERS or Glass Eels were a seasonal delicacy among the Foresters. They have been fished from the Rivers Severn, Wye and their tributaries for hundreds of years. They are remarkable little creatures, spawned in the Sargasso Sea in the North Atlantic who then undertake a three-year journey to reach Britain. If they are lucky, they grow into adult eels!

'Glass Eels' or Elvers

For most in the Forest, they were a free, cheap meal, full of protein. On a dark night, around the time of the first spring high tide, the Severn and Wye would be lit by hundreds of lights along both banks, each one marking the location of an angler with his box-like dip net ready to scoop up the fish as they swam in.

The Elver population has greatly dwindled over the last 40 years and so there are now strict restrictions on who can fish them and where.

Elver fishing at night – Gloucestershire Archives

A local poet F W Harvey wrote a poem about this Forest
favourite:

Up the Severn River from Lent to Eastertide
Millions and millions of slithy elvers glide,
Millions, billions of glassy bright
Little wormy fish,
Chewed-string fish,
Slithery dithery fish,
In the dead of night.

Up the gleaming river miles and miles along
Lanterns burn yellow: old joke and song
Echo as fishermen dip down a slight
Wide frail net,
Gauzy white net,
Strong long net
In the water bright.
From the Severn river at daybreak come
Hundreds of happy fishermen home
With bags full of elvers: perhaps that's why
We all love Lent
Lean mean Lent,
Fishy old Lent,
When the elvers fry.

When elvers fry for breakfast with egg chopped small
And bacon from the side that's hung upon the wall.
When the dish is on the table how the children shout
"Oh, what funny fish,
Wormy squirmy fish,
Weeny white fish,
Our mother's dishing out!"

Eels have a flavour (and a baddish one) of oil.
"When we have shuffled down their mortal coil,
What dreams may come!" what horrid nightmares neigh,
Gallop or squat,
Trample or trot,
Vanishing not
Till break of day!

"Never start nothing," says the motto in our pub:
"It might lead to summat": that's (as Shakespeare said) the rub!
So I'm not going to tell you, anyway not yet,
If the elvers are eels,
White baby eels,
Tiny shiny eels,
Caught with a net –

Or another quite separate wriggly kind of grub,
For I've seen more fights over that outside a pub
Than ever you saw at Barton Fair when Joe
The brown gipsy man,
The tawny gipsy man,
The tipsy gipsy man,
Tried to smart up the show.

But anyway, good people, you may search the river over
Before a breakfast tastier or cheaper you discover
Than elvers, and if all the year the elver season lasted
I wouldn't mind a bit,
I wouldn't care a bit,
Not a little tiny bit,
How long I fasted!

(ELVERS by F W Harvey published in his
Collected Poems 1912-1957 by Douglas McLean 1983)

Elvers tended to be served simply and plainly, quickly cooked to preserve the freshness of the fish, but when funds allowed they would be made into a more interesting dish. I spoke to an elderly lady about her memories of elvers and she recalled how as a toddler she used to cringe when her dad brought home a bucket of the horrible wriggly, slimy creatures. She remembered that one time the dog tipped over the bucket and the slithery eels spilled all over the floor and she screamed and climbed onto a chair to get away from the ugly things! However, she did recall how tasty they were once her mam had cooked them with some bacon and eggs!

ELVERS GLOUCESTERSHIRE-STYLE is very much like a breakfast dish.

1lb Elvers   *2 rashers of bacon (Glos Old Spot)*   2 eggs

Scour the Elvers several times in salt water. Cook the bacon in a frying pan and remove. Replace with Elvers. Break 2 eggs into pan and cook until Elvers turn a consistent white. Serve with bacon and a dash of vinegar.

Elvers were also served like whitebait, lightly coated in seasoned flour and deep fried

ELVER CHEESE was a medieval favourite.

Wash and boil Elvers. Press into a small greased dish. Will be a greenish-white colour. Turn out and slice as required. Finish by frying in bacon fat or lard.

Salmon– wikipedia

The River Severn is also home to **SALMON** a fish that has always been an important part of the Foresters' diet and the catching of them in the Rivers Severn and Wye is a longstanding tradition. For generations fishermen have used a Y-shaped frame with netting known as 'Lave Nets' which were either used from boats or by simply wading out into the dangerous waters. Salmon were also and are still trapped in funnel-shaped willow and hazel baskets called 'Putchers' placed in a 'hedge', 'rank' or 'leader' barrier across the flowing rivers. Unfortunately, these forms of fishing have almost died out due to dwindling stocks, EU regulations, and Health and Safety issues. A

2016 court case saw a Lydney Salmon fisherman given the right to claim damages after his 650 basket putcher rank in the River Severn was restricted to catching 30 salmon a season, instead of the 600 prior to 2011.

Lave Net Fishing – Gloucester Archives

SALMON recipes from back in the day are very few as generally the fish would have been cooked over an open fire or salted, smoked or dried to preserve for future use. In 1308, Edward II requisitioned 3000 dried salmon from the Rivers Severn and Wye to feed his troops in Scotland to show the opposition that England had just as good salmon as the Scots!

The Reverend Edward Davies (1718-89), a Welsh writer and Anglican priest, wrote a recipe in rhyme in 1786 called *Chepstow: a poem in six cantos,* in which he shows salmon are easy to cook:-

> ... *Adown the back the cook the fish divides*
> *Take out the chine, in pieces cut the sides;*
> *Plung'd in the coldest water let it lie*
> *Till the pot boils, and foaming, bubbles high:*
> *Then piece by piece he souses in the fish,*
> *Which, boiled ten minutes, makes the kings a dish* ...

William Makepeace Thackeray visited the area in 1842 and wrote that the River Wye salmon was the best salmon that was ever eaten in the world and that if it was eaten with a little salt and a slice of bread; it was then "unforgettable joy". He also described the Chepstow salmon as worth its weight in gold and far finer than those fished in the Taff, Tyne or Tweed!

Shad (Alosa Alosa) – Britishseafishing.co.uk

Another common fish found in the local rivers was the SHAD, a miserable fish of the herring family. Apparently tasteless and bony, but free, they provided many Foresters with a filling meal. The amazing Twaite Shad enters a river to reproduce each May, hence the local name of "May fish". They were so predictable that you could set your calendar by their arrival. Apparently, they are now a protected species.

A large catch of SHAD would be deheaded, detailed, gutted, and then thrown into a rapidly boiling copper, normally used for the weekly wash. This would apparently fill the house with an undesirable stench! Salt, pepper, bay leaves and other herbs would be added and when the cauldron was once again boiling the fire would be extinguished and the fish would be left to steep until cold. The fish would be replaced in the pot by potatoes, which would be cooked. Meanwhile the fish would be deboned and skinned. Once cooked the potatoes would be joined by large blocks of butter, the fish, parsley and other secret herbs and seasonings and then be all mashed together. A little milk would be added to get the right consistency to form palm-sized fishcakes. These were then egged and rolled in stale breadcrumbs, ready to be fried on a griddle. A quantity this size could feed a village or two!

Some Forest women would make these large batches and then sell them to neighbours and grocers to earn a few extra pennies.

DINNER IS SERVED!

———◦———

Most of the following recipes are from dishes that used local produce that the Foresters grew and reared themselves or in the case of the next recipe, caught themselves!

ROOK PIE sounds rather like a nursery rhyme dish but was seriously eaten if money was short. Rooks were seen as pests, supposedly eating newly sewn seed or corn and many a farmer would take his gun to them. In 1844, the Gloucester Journal reported a public

The Rook (Corvus Frugilegus) – rspb.org.uk

meeting had been held to discuss how to keep Rook numbers down, blaming them for decimating wheat, beans and potatoes. In 1948, the paper again wrote about a war on Rooks and it was even muted that Army Cadets could use the birds for target practice. The fact that Rooks are insectivores was neither here or there and in times of hardship and conflict, they featured on many menus. It is said that Rook shooting is one of Gloucestershire's oldest traditions and many pubs in the county still host annual Rook Pie Nights! The recipes at these establishments are a little grander than the Foresters used to cook, with brandy and sherry complimenting the meat. It is alleged that the nursery rhyme featuring four and twenty blackbirds is in fact referring to rooks, who are of course black birds! Who knows?

An 1860 recipe in *Cassell's Dictionary of Cookery* book describes rooks as having a dry and coarse flesh that requires long, slow stewing. Later cookery books state that only young rooks should be eaten.

1 rook per person   Onions, herbs, water, milk   Pie crust.

An uncooked Rook Pie!

Soak the rooks overnight in milk to remove any bitter taste having defeathered, skinned, gutted and removed the backbone. Poach in water with the onions and herbs slowly. Before finished, cover with a piecrust. Sometimes the pie was served with the bird's feet sticking out of the crust!

It is said that young rooks taste a little like squabs, but I am not overly keen to catch any to try! Catching them might be the problem!

Having mentioned Squabs, the next dish SQUAB PIE does not however involve any birds despite its title. In the Forest and its environs, lamb is the major ingredient. This is a dish that has a very medieval element; the use of spices and fruit with meat, very much the trend by chefs today in the twenty-first century!

Forest of Dean Commoners lamb –
Commoners Association

The Forest of Dean has long been associated with sheep rearing, either on the farm or, in particular, on common land, so lamb and mutton were always common sources of protein. The river valleys in the area were home to countless orchards, which provided a ready crop of apples that compliment this dish.

There are two versions of this recipe, one with leftover lamb, the other with fresh cuts. The former with a potato / swede topping, the latter with a shortcrust pastry topping. Take your choice, they are both delicious!

1½ lbs lamb neck fillets	or	1 lb leftover lamb
2 onions finely sliced		1 lb potatoes
1 large cooking apple, peeled and sliced		8 ozs swede, boiled & mashed together
½ teaspoon all spice		2 onions finely sliced
½ teaspoon nutmeg		1 large cooking apple, peeled & sliced
¼-pint lamb or vegetable stock		¼-pint lamb or vegetable stock
8 ozs shortcrust pastry		½ teaspoon all spice
Salt & pepper, egg to glaze		½ teaspoon nutmeg
		Salt & pepper + knob of butter

Preheat oven to 200°C / 400°F / Gas 6.

In a greased deep dish layer the lamb, then apple and onion, sprinkling each time with a little of the seasoning and spices. Repeat one more time. Pour over stock and then top with either the pastry or potato / swede topping. Glaze pastry with egg, dot knobs of butter over the mash.

For the pastry pie, bake in oven for 20 minutes then reduce heat to 180°C / 350°F / Gas 4 for 1 hour.

OLD GLOUCESTER CATTLE AT COTSWOLD FARM PARK

For the mash topped pie, bake in oven for 50 minutes until golden brown.

Gloucester Cattle at Cotswold Park Farm
– Jenny Care collection

Gloucester Cattle are an ancient breed, numerous in the Severn Vale as early as the 13th century. They were valued for their milk, which was used in cheese making, their meat, and for providing strong, draught oxen. However, by 1972, because of changing farm techniques and the introduction of other breeds, there was only one herd remaining in the country. Luckily, the breed has been saved from total extinction and there are now over 700 females registered. The animal is strikingly beautiful. The body is a dark mahogany colour with black legs and head. A white stripe passes from the small of the back, over the tail and down under the udder to cover the belly. The picture is completed by the mid-length, up-sweeping horns, white with black tips that adorn the head.

The mash-topped squab pie is very much like a Shepherd's Pie with 'knobs on', which leads us neatly onto

COTTAGE PIE. The beef used in this recipe would have originally been from local Gloucester Cattle along with bacon from the Gloucester Old Spot pig.

1 lb minced cold beef	8 ozs cold mashed potato
4 ozs minced cold bacon	1 beaten egg
2 onions diced	4 ozs fresh breadcrumbs
1 oz butter	Salt & pepper
Leftover gravy	

Season the beef and bacon. Fry onions in butter. Add the gravy and bring to the boil. Mix the egg, meat, bacon, potatoes and breadcrumbs thoroughly together and add to the gravy. Turn into a greased oven dish and bake in an oven at 180°C / 350°F / Gas 4 for 30 minutes. Leave to cool.

Traditionally this was served cold with a basic salad. Very much like a meatloaf!

Gloucester Old Spot Pig –
Smarts Dairy

PIGS were very common in the Forest, once upon a time, often seen roaming loose. This was known as the *Right to Pannage*. Pigs owned by free men were allowed to roam freely in the Forest of Dean in the autumn, ridding the ground of green acorns, which are poisonous to horses, ponies and cattle, and beech nuts. The right dates back to the 'Charter of the Forest', issued on 6th November 1217 during the reign of Henry III., which stated that *"We grant that every free man can conduct his pigs through our demesne wood freely and without impediment to agist them in his own woods or anywhere else he wishes. And if the pigs of any free man shall spend one night in our forest he shall not on that account be so prosecuted that he loses anything of his own"*. Unfortunately, today in the 21st century, this right has been overtaken by the unlawful release of boar, which means it is now unsafe to let pigs graze in unfenced territory!

Most families kept a pig, more than likely a Gloucester-shire Old Spot. They were bred to survive on the whey by-product from cheese making, acorns and windfall apples foraged in the forest, which is probably why they have the nickname 'Orchard Pig'. Shaped like a huge artillery shell with no discernible neck, and with large floppy ears it is surprisingly a very docile, hardy creature. The meat is well flavoured and with a good layer of fat, which lends itself to producing top quality crackling. As Winifred Foley remarks in her autobiography *Full Hearts & Empty Bellies* (1974) "Pigs were regarded practically as neighbours. They had their own stone dwellings along-side the cottages and were christened with pretty names like Rosie, Sukey or Ginny". When the pig was slaugh-tered, its blood went into Black Pudding, the feet were rendered for lard, and the big side-flitch was salted and hung in the living room to cure in the smoke from the open fire. Bacon and hams were produced, trotters boiled, intestines made into chitterlings, in fact hardly a single part of the animal was wasted, even the bladder was inflated to make a football! Joyce Latham wrote a poem about her Forest childhood experiences with the family pig:

BACON BUTTY

From an iron hook they hung him
Upside-down, an awesome sight,
When a draught so slowly swung him,
Oh! It gave me such a fright.
Draped around the victim's torso
Hung a veined, translucent veil,
From his head, which scared me more so,
Blood dripped down into a pail.
Then a wooden bench scrubbed cleanly
Helped to bear the corpse's weight
And the butcher, no way meanly,
Chopped him up – Oh, what a fate!
Ham and bacon he divided,
With saltpetre they were cured,
Then upon a nail provided
To the wall they were secured.

Lumps of fat to lard were turning
In a pan upon the hob.
For those scrutchins I was yearning,
Crisp and crunchy – just the job!
Spare ribs, griskin, lights and liver,
Pale pink trotters boiled with peas,
Red blood, oozing like a river,
Made black puddings for our teas.

Home-made faggots, so delicious,
Food galore for many a meal,
What a pig! Oh, so nutritious,
Nothing wasted but the squeal!

(JOYCE LATHAM – published in her autobiography Where I Belong by Alan Sutton Publishing 1993)

Once the pig was jointed, there was usually the backbone left and this was used in a meal the whole family looked forward to – LAZARUS BONE PIE.

Boil chunks of backbone with a chopped onion and some seasoning. Cool and transfer to a pie dish. Add a little of the liquid the bones were cooked in. Cover with a short-crust pastry. If the pie is to be eaten cold, add some gelatine to the liquid. Cook in a moderate over until the crust is golden brown. This was often eaten as a supper dish on the family's return from church.

Another popular meal in the Forest made from cheap cuts of meat was FORESTER'S FAGGOTS, which used the Pig's Brace or Fry as the major ingredient. To make a perfect faggot it was important to buy the Brace or Fry with the Caul. I had to use the internet to interpret this strange language! A Pig's Fry or Brace is the offal of the pig including the liver, heart, lungs, spleen, lights and sweetbreads. The Caul is the membrane that surrounds the abdomen.

1½ lbs Pig's Fry	3 large Onions
¼ lb Bacon	10 sprigs finely chopped Sage
2 lbs Breadcrumbs	Salt and Pepper

Mince offal, bacon and onions. In a large bowl, mix the offal, bacon, onions with breadcrumbs, sage and seasoning. Make mixture into balls and wrap each one in a small piece of caul. Place in buttered ovenproof dish

Faggots – Wikipedia

and cook for about 1 hour on a moderate heat. Turn faggots over halfway through cooking to prevent crusting on one side. Foresters would probably have cooked these in a pan on top of the stove. A crusty exterior was a bonus, adding flavour to the meal.

Faggots are still a favourite in the Forest and can be found in the butcher's shops alongside chitterlings and black pudding.

Another use of the Fry was PIG'S FRY PASTY.

1 lb Pig's Fry + Caul	1 large Onion
3 medium Potatoes	boiling water
Salt and Pepper	Sage

Wash the fry, except for the caul. Place a layer of sliced fry in a stewpot, then some slices of potato, onion and season. Continue to build the layers until all ingredients have been used. Pour enough boiling water over the layers to cover them. Place the caul over the mixture and cook in a very moderate oven for 2½ hours.

So far the recipes written have used most parts of the pig that today's home cooks and chefs would ignore and perhaps only used to flavour stocks and gravies. This last pig recipe is no different.

Another very old recipe and one not commonly cooked today in the home is HEADCHEESE; showing once again that every part of the pig was used to feed the family. It is also known as Brawn.

A head of a pig is involved but there is no cheese! The pig's head is singed to burn off bristles and whiskers. It is then soaked in salt water for 24 hours. Once removed from the water it is scrubbed to remove all remaining bristles and hairs. To remove bristles and hair in nostrils and ears a red-hot poker should be thrust into the animal's orifices!

Headcheese – Wikipedia

The head is placed in a large pan and covered with cold water. A few bay leaves, bunch of parsley, sage and thyme are added with a handful of summer savoury. Two or three onions and two carrots, cut into pieces, join them in the pot. A muslin bag of peppercorns and a few cloves are also added to the fusion.

The pot is brought to the boil and left to simmer for at least three hours or until meat is cooked (In reality it can take up to 24 hours). The tongue takes the longest time to cook so once that is tender the rest is cooked.

The meat is strained and, once cool, the head and tongue are skinned and the cooked meat is picked off. In a lined loaf tin, the pieces of meat are placed and some of the stock, to which has been added a tablespoon of white vinegar is poured over the mixture, just to moisten the terrine. (When cooled the stock will congeal because of the natural collagens found in the skull. If it doesn't start to jellify as it cools, boil and reduce by half. Still no joy then add some gelatine.) Once the loaf tin is full of meat, stock, and parsley if desired, the tin is covered with muslin or greased paper and a plate and weight are placed on top. It is then left in the fridge to chill at least overnight.

Please note that the eyes of the pig, which will have fallen out of their sockets during boiling, can be thrown to the hens! (Chops the ears and add to the other meat.)

Once fully set it can be sliced and used in sandwiches or salads.

WESTBURY PIE is another cheap, filing meal that may have been introduced around wartime, possibly because of the large numbers of US soldiers that were billeted in the Forest. They brought with them their own supplies of American food and many of these delicacies made their way into Forest homes!

Make shortcrust pastry to line a 7" pie plate. Put to one side enough pastry to form a lid. Slice a small tin of spam or luncheon meat. Lay over the base of the pastry. Whisk two eggs with a ¼ pint milk and salt and pepper and poor over meat. Dampen the edges of the pastry and place lid on top. Brush with milk. Cook in a moderately hot oven for ten minutes and then down to a moderate heat and cook for a further 25 minutes or until golden brown.

For the vegetarians, though in reality it was for the really poor who couldn't afford meat, AG PAG DUMP was a common, economical, filling meal made with some rather unusual ingredients. 'Dump' means a steamed or boiled pudding, which could be savoury or sweet. If one was fortunate, a few scraps of bacon or meat might be added!

1 teacupful of Barley boiled until soft	10 Blackcurrant leaves
1 bunch Dandelion leaves	2 Onions
1 small bunch Watercress	1 small bunch Sorrel leaves
Sprigs of Mint, Thyme and Sage	
1 Egg + tablespoon Butter	Salt and Pepper

Wash and chop the greens finely and then add to barley with a pinch of salt and pepper. Add meat if have any. Beat an egg and water with the butter and add to barley mix. Either place in a cloth or boil in a pot with a cabbage! Or steam for 1½ hours in a buttered basin. Serve with gravy and in the twenty-first century some braised beef!!

As many people know, the Forest of Dean is inhabited by other members of the SUIDAE or PORCINE family – WILD BOAR. They were very common in the forest in the thirteenth century, hunted for the kings table. There is a record of an order for 100 boars and sows for a Christian feast in 1254, where they were simply roasted on a spit. Because they were deemed a royal preserve anyone caught poaching and eating such animals were liable to heavy penalties, including death. Boar were often a symbolic centrepiece for many medieval celebrations, from a coronation to a religious festival. They are even celebrated in a song from the fourteenth century:

> *The Boar's head in hand I bring*
> *With garlands gay in carrying,*
> *I praye you all with me to sing*
> *Hey! Hey! Hey! Hey!*

Forest Boar – Paul Williams

The animal gradually died out in the Forest through over hunting but were reintroduced in the seventeenth century, but were then seen as pests and were hunted to extinction.

In the late twentieth century, the forest became home once again to the Boar as a couple of farmers decided to rear the animal for its meat. However, whether by accident or on purpose the boar escaped their confines in the 1990s and since then have lived freely in the Forest. As of early 2019 rumours say there are some 2000 roaming despite an annual cull carried out by the Forestry Commission. The meat from the culls finds its way into local shops and restaurants and I can attest that Boar sausages are very tasty either grilled or barbecued. The meat is lean and tender, but overcooking can make it tough. Slow cook joints (15-20 minutes per kg) at about 180° or Gas 4, though over a spit is more traditional.

VENISON features alongside Boar as another royal preserve back in medieval times. It is reported that William the Conqueror was hunting in the Forest of Dean in 1089 when he heard the Danes had captured York. Deer were very plentiful in the Forest for centuries but were off limits to Forest dwellers and were protected by laws upheld by the Forest Verderers. However, the deer population became so depleted through over-hunting that by 1855 there were none left in the Forest. They were reintroduced after WWII, with today the Forest housing not only Fallow Deer, but some Roe and Muntjac as well. Few recipes exist for venison dishes; obviously, because only the privileged ate it and Foresters were not going to admit to cooking Venison for fear of reprisals, such as emasculation or blinding. Even today, it still holds the mystique of being a posh foodstuff! However many butcher shops can be found selling it as burgers or steaks.

If the monarch should be in the Forest and was lucky enough to kill some deer, then he might be served his trophy as BROILED or BAKED VENISON or VENISON CUSTARDE or ROO BROTH.

BROILED VENISON was a popular meat dish served at medieval banquets and feasts. The animal was scored, parboiled, and then larded before being spit roasted. A basting sauce of red wine and ground ginger would be poured over during the cooking to add extra flavour and richness.

BAKED VENISON was an oven-cooked dish that can be cooked today. It was cooked as a pie flavoured with spices, one of which may be a little difficult to obtain today – Grains of Paradise.

Grains of Paradise is the common name for the seeds of the *Aframomum Melegueta* which is an herbaceous perennial plant native to West Africa with trumpet-shaped purple flowers that develop into long pods containing reddish-brown seeds that give a pungent, peppery taste with a hint of citrus. It is also known as Melegueta pepper or Alligator pepper.

VENISON CUSTARDE was a Venison stew flavoured with spices such as saffron, ginger and cinnamon cooked in wine with added dates and prunes and verjuice. Once cooked the juices when cooled were thickened with eggs and then the whole dish was reheated to cook the eggs. Verjuice is a highly acidic juice made from pressing unripe grapes, crab apples or other sour fruit. It is still used in South America apparently!

ROO BROTH was not a Kangaroo soup! It was more like a stew made with the liver of the Deer and other cheaper cuts of the animal. It would be boiled in equal measures of water and red wine. Once parboiled bread that had been soaked in the blood of the deer would be added. Also added was ginger, cinnamon, mace and a large measure of

Fresh Forest Venison! –
Forest of Dean & Wye Valley Tourist Board

vinegar and currants, which would then be simmered until the venison was fully cooked. Later versions of this recipe saw the addition of onions and herbs. The sweetness of the onions and herbs was to counterbalance the sharpness of the vinegar, an ingredient that was common in mediaeval venison recipes as it was and is a great tenderiser of tough cuts of meat.

A couple of animals I have not mentioned are rabbits and chickens, two ingredients one would think would have featured highly in a Forester's diet.

RABBITS are not an indigenous creature in the British Isles, and were deliberately introduced from Europe, probably by the Normans. There is definite evidence they were present in the late 12th and early 13th centuries, though not necessarily. in the Forest of Dean. In fact, rabbits found the British climate inhospitable and so required careful rearing and cosseting, their meat and fur being very valuable for their

Westbury Court 20th Century Rabbit Warren
– National Trust

owners: the owners being the monarchy and landed gentry! The rabbits or 'coneys' were raised in warrens or 'coneygarths' which were man-made barrows in a defined area, protected by pales, walls, hedges, fences or natural watercourses. Poaching from such a warren resulted in stern penalties.

It was not until the 17th century that we find a record of a warren on the Forest side of the river Severn. The Colchester family at Westbury Court, Westbury-on-Severn built a large warren in their grounds, which provided them with plenty of fresh meat and fur, to adorn their clothes and provide warm garments for the winter months. It is quite possible that some poaching did take place, but there are no records of actual recipes that the Foresters might have followed, though they probably would have been quite simple.

One such dish might have been RABBIT in BROTH or CONNYNGES in SYRUP. This meal was a simple stew. The rabbit would be cut into pieces then parboiled in a 'Gode Broth', A 'Gode Broth' was a mixture of chicken and pork stock with added breadcrumbs, pepper and salt, cumin, saffron, ground almonds, sugar and ginger. When the rabbit meat started to fall from the bone, the dish was ready to eat.

CHICKENS were a common bird, found in most Forest homes back yards: kept for their eggs and then once too old to lay, their meat.

There seem to be no special recipes involving chicken. FOREST CHICKEN was similar to Squab Pie, but with cooked chicken instead of lamb, topped with mashed potatoes and swede. In addition, I have found a similar recipe to Rabbit in Broth, this time 'CHECONYS' in SYRUP!

SAY CHEESE!

———◦———

It is said that back in the day the Gloucestershire labouring man's staple food when working in the fields or down the mines was crusty bread, an onion and a lump of cheese washed down with rough cider or cold tea. This was known as a 'Snowle'. The cheese was an important ingredient of a meal due to its high calorific value, which gave the worker energy, and strength for the day's labours.

Mention Gloucestershire when talking about cheese and the words Double Gloucester come tumbling of the tongue. The cheese originally made in the Severn Vale was from the milk of Cotswold sheep. So much cheese was produced from the animals that grazed on the lush area that in 1498 a permanent cheese market was set in Eastgate Street, Gloucester (the site of today's indoor market).

By Tudor times, cow's milk became the norm for cheese making, especially from the Old Gloucester cattle, as their milk with its high fat globules and high protein levels made a fine textured cheese. By 1789, it is recorded that Gloucestershire was producing some 1000 tonnes of cheese a year all from Old Gloucester Cattle milk. By the nineteenth century, this cheese production almost ended as more fresh milk was being sold to drink rather than for producing other dairy foodstuffs. As the cheese making died so did the Old Gloucester cattle and by the 1970s was almost extinct.

The late twentieth century saw a turnaround in the cheese and cattle fortunes as everything organic and local became the latest fad and today there is a thriving cheese industry in the county with three speciality cheeses making their mark using the Old Gloucester cattle milk; Single Glouces-ter, Double Gloucester and thanks to *Wallace & Gromit*, Stinking Bishop. The Single Gloucester cheese was given protected designation of origin status (PDO) in 1996.

Single Gloucester is not a cheese widely heard of outside of Gloucestershire but that is probably because of how it is made. Unpasteurised full cream milk from the morning milking and skimmed milk from the evening milking plus vegetable rennet, is used to produce this once purely home-made cheese that was for family consumption and rarely for sale. Today it is made in bigger quantities,

Single & Double Gloucester Cheeses from Smarts Dairy, Churcham

but is still only left to mature for three weeks, which gives it a light texture with a cool, clean tang and grassy flavour and thereby because of its youth it does not travel well.

Double Gloucester, the more famous cheese, was origi-nally made to provide the household with an income. It is made from vegetable rennet and unpasteurised full cream milk from both the morning and evening milkings with added annatto, a natural dye derived from seeds of the achiote tree, to produce the orange-red colour. Originally, the cheese was coloured with beetroot or carrot juice and even the flower known as 'Lady's Bedstraw' (Galium Verum) which gave the cheese a distinctive yellow colour. The cheese is aged for a minimum of six months, which allows it to be sold all over the world. It is rich, mellow, powerful and earthy, slightly crumblier than cheddar. Because it is harder and more robust than Single Glouces-ter, it is an ideal for 'Cheese Rolling'! Every Whit Monday (or Spring Bank Holiday today) at Cooper's Hill, Glouces-ter, four large cheeses are rolled down a steep hill with a merry crowd in pursuit. This dangerous activity is said to have derived from the need to maintain grazing rights on the common – whatever the history it now attracts 'eccentrics' from all over the world!

Most Gloucestershire cheese recipes use Double Glouces-ter due to its rich flavour so if the recipe just says cheese, read Double Gloucester.

FORESTERS CHEESE & ALE is a regional version of the Welsh Rarebit.

8 ozs Double Gloucester	1 teaspoon English Mustard
½ pint Brown Ale	8 thick slices of toasted Bread

Slice cheese thinly and place in a buttered dish. Spread mustard evenly over cheese. Pour brown ale over cheese and cover dish with foil. Bake for 10 minutes at 375°F/190°C/Gas 5 until cheese is softened. Pour cheese and ale mixture over toast and serve piping hot.

Sounds a little messy but rather tasty!

Potting is one of the oldest English means of preserving. Grated, minced or pounded protein would be enthusiastically seasoned and set in a base of equal amounts of butter and protein. A crust of clarified butter would seal the top to keep the bacteria at bay (ordinary butter spoils faster because of fat solids).

POTTED CHEESE is one such traditional preserved dishes that, from its ingredients, is unlikely to have been for the labourers table!

½ lb grated Cheese	½ lb unsalted Butter
2 tablespoons Port, Red Wine or Sherry	¼ teaspoon Cayenne Pepper
¼ Mace	½ teaspoon dry Mustard
Splash of Worcestershire Sauce	melted clarified Butter

Pound all the ingredients together, then press into pots and cover with clarified butter. Twenty-first century addition: put in refrigerator for 24 hours for flavours to combine. Serve with toast or crackers.

I would suggest this was definitely a middle to upper class recipe! The following recipe would more than likely suit the finances of the poor!

FORESTERS CHEESE AND ONION POT Using fresh spring onions, allow about ½ a bunch per person. Chop these quite small and set to one side. Grate some Double Gloucester cheese allowing about 2 – 3 ozs per person. Combine the cheese and chopped onions together. Make a dressing of vinegar, salt and pepper and mix into the cheese mixture. Place the mix into individual serving dishes and serve with fresh bread and butter or a crusty French loaf.

CHEESE STEW is another tummy filler that makes an ideal supper dish.

1 lb Potatoes	½ pint milk
3 Onions	8 ozs Cheese
Salt and Pepper	

Peel and slice the potatoes thinly and place in milk in saucepan. Season and simmer until almost tender (about 10 minutes). Remove potatoes from milk and set aside. Chop onions finely. In a greased ovenproof casserole layer potatoes, onions and cheese, seasoning each layer with salt and pepper. End with a cheese layer. Pour milk over layers. Bake uncovered at 350°F/180°C/Gas 4 for about 1 hour until top is golden brown.

To finish off this course there is another simple recipe that was common in the Forester's repertoire and used up stale bread and the last of the cheese – CHEESE PUDDING.

3 ozs grated Cheese	2 ozs Breadcrumbs
½ pint Milk	½ oz Butter
1 or 2 Eggs	Salt and Pepper

Bring milk to the boil and pour over breadcrumbs. Add butter and leave to cool. Stir in cheese and well-beaten eggs. Season to taste. Pour into a greased pie dish and bake for 45 minutes or until golden brown at 375°F/190°C/Gas 5.

SWEET TOOTH!

——◆◇◆——

I shall now turn to the dessert menu – my favourite part of any meal!

Pancakes are a staple food in the culinary history of nearly every British county and in the past were a filler that a mere pittance of a wage could afford. Most of us of course have been brought up with their religious connections with Shrove Tuesday still marking the eve of Lent when rich foods such as fats, milk, sugar and eggs are used up before the period of fasting and pancakes are an easy way of using such foodstuffs.

FOREST PANCAKES in the Forest are a little different to the norm because they are more like Welsh Cakes or Griddle Cakes. They feature both suet and lard in their preparation, two ingredients that would need to be used up before Lent. This made the pancakes highly calorific, so at any time of year they helped fuel the labours of the agricultural workers who often carried them to work to eat cold. The pancakes have an unusual texture, variously described as sandy or grainy and they are about 2-3" in diameter.

3ozs finely grated Suet	1 Egg
1 dessertspoon Milk	6 ozs Flour
Pinch Salt	1 tablespoon Baking Powder
Lard	

Mix together the suet, flour, salt and baking powder. Beat the egg with the milk and then add to the dry mix to form a stiff paste. Turn out dough onto a floured board and roll out to approximately 1" thickness. Cut into rounds of about 2-3" in

Forest Pancakes – from Neil Cooks Grigson

diameter. Fry in hot lard until well cooked and a nice brown colour. Serve with syrup, jam or lashings of butter!

Until modern cookers, these would have been cooked on a bakestone on the fire or range.

FORESTERS TART was another easy pudding that was basic but nurturing.

Pastry to line a deep pie plate	4 ozs sugar
2 ozs butter	4 ozs currants
1 egg	

Line a deep pie plate with the pastry. Melt the butter, add all the other ingredients, and mix well. Pour the mixture into the pastry shell and bake in a moderate oven until golden brown.

Very much a Forest dessert is SPEECH HOUSE PUDDING. Reputedly the pudding was served to Charles II at The Speech House when he used it as a hunting lodge. The ingredients were those demanded of an English winter and the dessert was created to reward those who trampled through the frosty forest pursuing game. It is a steamed pudding originally cooked in a muslin cloth, very sweet and filling but remarkably light. The following recipe was supplied by The Speech House.

2 Eggs	2 ozs softened Butter
1 oz Caster Sugar	2 ozs Flour
1 large tablespoon Raspberry Jam	½ teaspoon Bicarbonate of Soda
1 tablespoon Milk	

Speech House Pudding
courtesy of pinterest.com

Grease a 2-pint pudding basin. Separate the eggs, whisk the whites until they are stiff, and form peaks. In a separate bowl beat the butter until it is light and creamy then beat in the egg yolks and sift in the flour. Fold carefully. Stir in the jam. Dissolve the bicarbonate of soda in the milk and fold into the mixture. Gently fold in the egg whites thoroughly and then transfer into the greased basin. It should be no more than three-quarters full. Cover the top with a piece of buttered, pleated grease-proof paper and then a piece of pleated foil, secured with string. Stand in a pan of boiling water for about 2-3 hours until well risen. DO NOT LET THE PAN GO DRY! Turn out and serve with a little hot jam.

Blakeney Red Pear

The Forest and its environs are well known for fruit orchards, the majority of fruit being used to produce drinks. In the village of Blakeney, the Blakeney Pear first grew and has a history going back as far as 1600. It is also known as the Red Pear, Circus Pear, Painted Lady or Painted Pear. It is a huge tree growing up to 50 feet tall and the pears glow red in the sunshine when they are ripe. It is renowned for making perry and especially a 'champagne' perry and it was once used to dye soldier's khaki uniforms but it can be used in desserts, as can other local pears, such as the Ciphrous, Early Hay and Green Roller pears from Westbury. This old recipe for PEAR PUFF can use any of the aforementioned pears.

Stew some peeled, cored pears in a little water in a saucepan. Add sugar to taste. When the pears begin to change colour drop a suet crust rolled to the size of the saucepan onto the pears and cook on a low heat for about 40 minutes. Serve with plenty of cream or custard.

A fruit that has been mentioned in many recipes is the APPLE, a prolific crop that was grown in the surround of the Forest, mainly for cider production. However, there were many varieties that were grown purely for dessert use. In Minsterworth, one could find Lemon Roy or

Reynold's Kernel, and in Walmore, one could find the Sugar Pippin or Tranparent Codlin growing.

The Transparent Codlin was especially good for simple BAKED APPLE dishes. It was medium sized; yellow skinned and when cooked, kept its shape. It was lemony and tangy, so filling the empty core area with sugar, dried fruit or jam was essential.

It was also very good for CRUSTED APPLES.

Apples	White of an Egg
Jam	Breadcrumbs
Mixture of Sugar and Ground Almonds	

Peel and core apples. Brush with the white of an egg. Fill the hole with homemade jam, then roll apples in sugar, and ground almond mixture. Bake in a fairly hot oven until light brown.

APPLE OMELETTE was a good way of using other cooking apples, such as Lemon Roy, Sugar Pippin or any windfalls that could not be wasted. Sour cider apples could also be used in this recipe. Lemon Roy was especially good for this dish. It was yellow in colour with a rich, citrus flavour. The texture was slightly dry and had a floury consistency when cooked.

1 lb Apples	1 oz Butter
2 ozs Breadcrumbs	1 Egg
2 ozs Sugar	½ Lemon

Peel, core, slice apples, and stew in sugar, butter and grated lemon rind until tender. Stir in a well-beaten egg. Put half the breadcrumbs in the bottom of a well-greased dish, pour over the apple mixture and then put the rest of the breadcrumbs on top. Dab with small pieces of butter and bake for 30 minutes in a moderate oven. Decorate with slices of apple.

BACHELOR'S PUDDING intimates it was for one person only, but could be doubled up depending on how many diners were present. Windfalls were ideal for this recipe.

Mix 2 ozs each of flour, breadcrumbs, currants, sugar, suet and grated or chopped apple. Add 1 egg, beaten with 2 tablespoons of milk. Pour into a greased bowl and steam for 2 hours.

Many dishes have evolved from religious festivals and HEG PEG DUMP is one such pudding from this area.

July 20th is the special day apparently of St Margaret of Antioch, the saint of safe childbirth, who was reportedly

St Margaret of Antioch – wikipedia

swallowed by a dragon, but was spat out unharmed because the wooden cross she carried upset the Dragon's digestive system! (The church at the Houses of Parliament is named St Margaret's in honour of her!) Forest folk revered St Margaret greatly in the medieval period and this dessert was cooked to celebrate her day.

It is basically a suet steamed pudding made from 'Heg Pegs' or wild plums found in the hedgerows – 'Heg'. It was more than likely chosen as a dish to celebrate the Saint because 'Peg' is the diminutive of Margaret! As for the word 'Dump' – as previously mentioned in this book, it is short for dumpling; therefore, Heg Peg Dump is a Suet Plum Pudding!

DOUGH	8 ozs Flour	4 ozs Suet
	¼ pint Water	1 tablespoon Baking Powder
	½ teaspoon Salt	
FILLING:	1 lb stoned Plums (Blaisdons the best)	8 ozs sliced cooking Apples
	6 ozs Sugar	1 tablespoon Cake crumbs
	1 tablespoon Water	

Mix the flour, suet, salt and baking powder together and add enough water to form a soft dough. Knead well until smooth in texture. Divide dough into two (one piece about two-thirds to line the basin and the other a third which will be the lid of the pudding). Line a well-greased 2-pint basin with the rolled out two-thirds of the suet pastry. Fill the basin with alternate layers of plums, apples and sugar and add the water. Roll out the remaining piece of suet pastry to fit the basin, moisten the edges, and press firmly into place. Cover the bowl with a pleated buttered, greaseproof piece of paper and then a pleated piece of foil and secure with string. Steam for 3 hours. DO NOT LET THE PAN GO DRY! Serve with custard or cream.

The Blaisdon Red plum, as mentioned in the above recipe, was originally a wild plum 'discovered' in a hedge by John Dowding of Tan House Farm, Blaisdon, in the latter part of the 19th century. About 100 years ago, there were around 500 acres of Blaisdons in the area, with plenty of orchards that provided the plums for jam producers, such as Robertsons.

Blaisdon Red Plum – slowfood.org.uk

The trees centred on Blaisdon, but also were found in Flaxley, Huntley, Littledean, Longhope, Minsterworth, Mitcheldean and Westbury on Severn. Unfortunately today the tree stock has greatly reduced, but Haylings Farm in Newnham has a thriving, small plantation of them. It is said that Blaisdon Reds were found in the Antarctic huts of the ill-fated Scott expedition in 1913, as it is reputed that the plums assist the body in combating the effects of extreme cold!

The trees are prolific fruiters, disease-resistant, growing to a height of about 20 feet. It is known as a true plum because it grows on its own rootstock. The fruit is perfectly acidic for jam making when harvested early, but if allowed to ripen until late August, it becomes sweet, tasty, and ideal for use in deserts.

*King and Queen Plum at Blaisdon
Plum Festival in the 1980s –*
Vic Woodman

In the 1980s, the village of Blaisdon decided to celebrate its famous fruit by holding Plum Festivals over the August Bank Holiday weekends. Three such events were held, the first in 1982, then 1984 and the last in 1988. There were art exhibitions, craft fairs, plum stalls and musical entertainment to woo the crowds and all monies raised went to the church and village hall. In 1982, £1600 was raised for much needed church repairs. For the first festival, a plum recipe book was produced with every conceivable way of using plums, including Blaisdon Plum Gin and Hot Blaisdon Plum Trifle.

Another suet pudding, common during times of hardship or war was VEGETABLE PLUM PUDDING. The potato was often found as an ingredient in Gloucestershire dessert recipes and very often carrots would be added due to their sweetness. This recipe uses both and an enormous amount of sugar but no plums!! It seems to me the amounts are large enough to feed an army!

1 lb cooked mashed Potatoes	8 oz cooked mashed Carrots
1 lb Flour	½ lb shredded Suet
¾ lb Sugar	1 lb Currants
1 lb Raisins	2 tablespoons Nutmeg
Pinch of Salt	

Mix all ingredients together. Place in a greased basin or pudding cloth and steam/boil for 3--- hours.

The following recipe is an alternative version, which cooks the pudding in the oven and is more a family-sized recipe.

POTATO PUDDING

8 ozs mashed floury Potatoes	2ozs Butter
2 beaten Eggs	Juice and zest from 1 Lemon
2 ozs Sultanas	2 ozs Sugar
2 ozs Butter	

Mix mashed potatoes, butter, eggs, sultanas, sugar and lemon juice and zest together. Pour into greased pie dish and bake in oven 350°F/180°C/Gas 4 for 40 minutes until the pudding is firm to the touch and lightly browned. Serve hot with custard or cream.

TIME FOR TEA!

We can now look at something tasty to have with a cup of tea or coffee at 'Elevenses' or 'Afternoon Tea'.

BLAKENEY FRITTERS is a misnomer. When I saw the name I expected a fried fish or meat recipe, but it turns out to be a biscuit, the Forest of Deans equivalent of 'Jammie Dodgers'! The recipe uses margarine but one can replace with butter to give it a richer flavour.

1½ ozs Margarine	1 oz Sugar
3 ozs Flour	1 Egg Yolk
1 Egg White (use for glazing)	

Mix ingredients together to form a paste. Roll into small balls (about 8-9) and place on a greased baking sheet. Make a dent in the middle of each ball with the end of a spoon. Brush with the beaten egg white. Bake slowly in a moderate oven until they are slightly

My poor attempt at Blakeney Fritters!

flattened and a golden brown colour. Before they are cooled, fill each indentation with jam.

I have personally cooked these and found after some practice that Gas 4 is the optimal temperature to cook them at.

The making of 'pure yeast' was quite a laborious chore in
Forest households, but necessary to make bread foodstuffs for the family. On a Monday morning, the
housewife would get 2 ozs of best hops and boil them in
a gallon of water for about 30 minutes. The washing
copper or a cauldron was ideal for this chore (once the
washing was done of course!). The liquid would then be
strained and cooled to body temperature and to this was
added a handful of salt and ½ lb of brown sugar. Into this
mixture was beaten 1 lb of best flour. The pot was left
next to the fire until Wednesday, frequently stirred. On
Wednesday, 2 lb of mashed potatoes were added and
thoroughly mixed in. The concoction was then left next to
the fire again to stand for a day, stirring frequently. On
Thursday, the liquid would be strained through a cloth
and poured into bottles. The bottles would be corked
tightly and then stored in a cool place for up to two
months. It was at its peak at the end of this period and
then was ready to make CHELTENHAM CAKES ensuring it
was shaken well before use.

The recipe for these cakes was probably brought to the
Forest by young girls, who during the Victorian period in
to the 20th century had to leave the Forest to find employment. Many, like the author Winifred Foley (*Full Hearts
and Empty Bellies* published by Abacus 2008) went into
service in the large houses found in this fashionable spa
town. The cakes were basically a sweet, rich bread roll that
could be eaten with a savoury filling such as cheese or a
sweet filling such as jam.

2 lb Flour	4 ozs Butter
1 pint warm Milk	2 Egg yolks
1 oz Yeast	

Melt the butter in the milk, then add all the other ingredients and mix thoroughly. Set to rise in a warm place for about an hour. Make the dough into round buns about 2-3" in diameter and leave to rise again. Bake in hot oven 400°F/200°C/Gas 6 for about 15 minutes.

LARDY CAKES were once a very popular regional dish, made with a yeast bun dough, dried fruit and lots of lard rendered from the Gloucester Old Spot family pig. It is still very popular in the Forest and is very much a comfort food but some recipes today have cut down on the use of lard and replaced it with butter. I have to agree with the great ELIZABETH DAVID, "How could they be Lardy Cakes without lard?" The following recipe was one I obtained from a member of the Bream Gardening Society:

DOUGH:	1 lb strong white Bread Flour	1 teaspoon Salt
	¼ oz Yeast	½ oz Lard
	½ pint lukewarm Milk	
FILLING:	5 ozs Lard	5 ozs Light Brown Sugar
	1 teaspoon Mixed Spice	7 ozs Mixed Dried Fruit
TIN:	1 oz Lard	2 tablespoons Light Brown Sugar
GLAZE:	1 tablespoon White Sugar	1 tablespoon Water

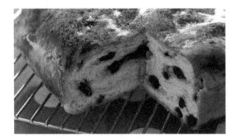

Lardy Cake – BBC.com

Put the flour and salt in a bowl and rub in lard. Mix in the yeast and then add the milk. Knead together for about 10 minutes until smooth and stretchy. Put the dough back in the bowl and cover with a damp tea towel and leave to rise in a warm place until it is about twice the size. When the dough is ready, knock back (knock the air out) and knead gently back into a ball. Roll the dough into a large rectangle. Dot $\frac{1}{3}$ rd of lard over $\frac{2}{3}$ rds of the dough (leave the top $\frac{1}{3}$ rd clear) then sprinkle over $\frac{1}{3}$ rd of the dried fruit and sugar and a little of the mixed spice. Fold the clear $\frac{1}{3}$ rd. down over the middle $\frac{1}{3}$ rd and then fold up the bottom $\frac{1}{3}$ rd up over the other two. Give the dough a half turn and roll out to a large rectangle like the one you started with. Repeat this procedure twice more, finally rolling out the dough to fit your tin. Place in the tin, which will have been heavily greased with lard and sprinkled with light brown sugar. Leave the dough to rise in a warm place.

Bake at 400°F/200°C/Gas 6 for 30 minutes until golden brown.

Before cake is taken out of the oven, make the glaze. Melt the sugar in the water and brush over cake immediately it comes out of the oven. Leave the cake for a maximum of 2 minutes in the tin before turning out. Any longer and it will stick!

A cheaper version of this cake was called SCRATCHING CAKE or SCRUTCHEON CAKE and was made in the poorer homes in the Forest. The pig fat (especially the leaf round the kidneys) once rendered down would leave crusty, fatty deposits in the pan and these were incorporated into a raw bread dough and then baked to produce a tasty fatty-style filling.

Another version of lardy cake is called DRIPS or DRIPPING CAKE. Instead of lard, the recipe uses beef dripping, usually made from the Old Gloucester Cattle meat joints. It is made just the same as the lardy cake though there is no glaze and the tray is greased with butter and brown sugar to produce a toffee-type covering. Because of this, the cake must be turned out of the tin immediately it comes out of the oven or it will stick.

DOUGH:	1 lb strong white Bread Flour	1 teaspoon Salt
	½ oz Beef Dripping	¼ oz Yeast
	½ pint lukewarm Milk	
FILLING:	5 ozs Lard	5 ozs Light Brown Sugar
	7 ozs Mixed Dried Fruit	1 teaspoon Mixed Spice
TIN:	3½ ozs butter	½ oz Light Brown Sugar

Make the Drips as per the Lardy Cake recipe but bake at 425°F / 220°C / Gas 7 for 40 minutes. The Drips will rise and go a dark brown. Turn out almost immediately it is removed from the oven. BE VERY CAREFUL AS THE TOFFEE SAUCE WILL BE VERY HOT!!

Some bakeries in the county would send out the trays of Drips to the retailers without turning them out. The shops would then cut the bake into squares and sell from the tray leaving the 'toffee sauce' at the bottom, crusty and sticky and the rest of the cake untouched by the sauce and so customers were invariably denied the best bit of the bake!

DUMB CAKES are something that one would probably not want to eat but ought to be mentioned, as they are part of the Forest's rich food heritage. Recipes for Dumb cakes can be found all over the country, the name deriving from the Middle English 'doom' meaning 'fate' or 'destiny'. They were cakes made on an auspicious day (St Marks' Eve – April 24th; St Agnes's Eve – January 20th; Midsummer's Eve or Halloween) by spinster maidens to discover their future husbands. In the Forest of Dean, an area

Print by W Finden c 1843 – making Dumb Cakes

largely untouched by religion due to the fact it was Crown Land and the monarchy connected churches with communities and did not want communities forming in the Forest, tended to celebrate this tradition on Christmas Eve. It was a very plain cake made by two or three maidens in absolute silence as the slightest sound would destroy the magic. The maidens would scratch their initials into the top of the cake then bake it in the ashes of the open range. The maidens would go to bed leaving the front door open and legend has it that their intended would then sneak into the house at midnight and add his initials to hers. The bond would then be sealed by the fair maidens eating the cake next morning.

To be honest looking at some of the recipes, the cake looks extremely inedible, so it must have been desperation to find true love that made the maiden eat the cake, but then whether the cake tasted good or not was irrelevant to the magic!

One formula for such a cake is:

An egg-shell-full of salt	An egg-shell-full of wheat meal
An egg-shell-full of barley-meal	Water

The rest of the country had even more bizarre rituals involving Dumb Cakes, some quite dark, but they all seemed to involve some form of inedible foodstuff!

CHEERS!

So what would Foresters have washed all this lovely food down with? There certainly used to be a large selection of drinks to choose from.

It is well known that the liquid of the choice in the South West has nearly always been a refreshing glass of CIDER or PERRY, and the Foresters would have enjoyed either or a mixture of the two. A Chronicler in 1601 observed that drinkers in the county of Gloucestershire were accustomed to 'be refreshed with great store of cider and perry'. Cider was even praised in 1630 as being 'a drink both pleasant and healthy', noted for its medicinal powers that 'cleanse the Stomach, strengthen the Diges-tion and free the Kidnies and Bladder from breeding the Gravel Stone'. The drink was taken on sea voyages and given to sailors, as it was deemed to prevent scurvy.

Bottle of cider

Bottle of perry

By 1800 it was used as a 'cure for a wide range of ills, including vomiting, gout, ailments of the urinary tract and rheumatic diseases' and it was noted that it was effective as a 'cleansing surgical dressing'. Perhaps it should be on prescription today!

The Forest and its environs were home to countless orchards, attached to either farms or private houses, where cider/perry would be produced and consumed at home, or in the case of farms, given to agricultural workers during their hard labours, but also as part payment of wages.

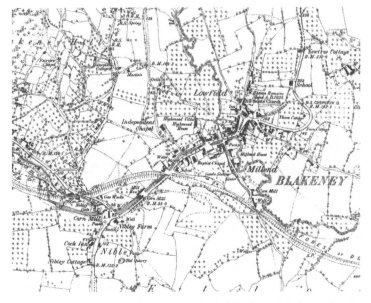

Orchards around Blakeney in 1893. There were countless individual orchards in the area shown by the many regular lines of trees.

These orchards could have been remnants of Roman habitation, for Romans developed cider making during their occupation of Britain, installing equipment that crushed the fruit and extracted the juice from their newly planted fruit groves along the banks of the rivers Wye and Severn.

The Styre apple – Gloucester Orchard Trust

Cider production in the Forest was enabled by the large number of apple varieties that were grown. The earliest variety was The Styre or Stire, which was an old English cider apple unique to the Forest; it grew well on the local thin, limestone soil, and produced a long-lasting, smooth yet deceptively strong drink. Other varieties that could be found were Blood Royal and Minsterworth Green, both from Minsterworth; Welsh Druid from Woolaston; Chaxhill Red from Chaxhill and Evan's Kernel from Ruardean – all of which made drinkable cider. Cider apples tend to be bittersweet, usually unpleasant to eat raw but contain a high level of tannins and sugar, which make them perfect to turn into a brew.

In the early days, farms and public houses would make enough cider to meet their own needs. They would use simple equipment to crush the fruit and extract the juice, such as small scratters, which would turn the fruit into a workable pomace for pressing. It is known that some public houses

A simple SCRATTER held at the Dean Heritage Centre, Forest of Dean. – Jenny Care

Cider Press – Jenny Care collection

owned their own orchards – such as The Miners Arms and Bell Beerhouse in Whitecroft. The building that once housed the Bell's cider press still remains, though the orchard and equipment are long gone! After a time some enterprising farmers in places like Awre and Westbury on Severn, saw the commercial possibilities of brewing cider and perry on a larger scale and so equipment was designed to make the drinks in larger quantities. Large stone mills were built and powered by horse or donkey to crush the fruit. Then the pulp was put in a press to extract every last drop of the juice. The liquid would then be left to brew, relying on the natural yeasts in the fruit to produce a still, cloudy, acidic, yet invigorating, thirst-quenching, potent beverage. This was called 'scrumpy' or 'rough cider'. Workers in the field would probably drink ½ a gallon for breakfast, the same for lunch and then more during their labours. It is surprising any work was done!

Large stone mill that would be operated by a horse or donkey. Held at Dean Heritage Centre, Forest of Dean. Jenny Care

It is said that before The Great War there were a couple of Forest pubs selling very potent cider and perry that went

Blakeney Red Pear Tree – Gloucester Orchard Trust

by the names of "Knock 'em Stiff" and "Stun 'em".

Perry making was centred on the Blakeney Red pear, the fruit of a large tree that could produce tonnes of fruit every year. The original 'wildings' or wild hybrids of pears were thought to have been brought to Britain, once again, by the Romans and at one time there were over 100 varieties, known by over 200 local names, in Gloucestershire alone. They included 'Stinking Bishop' well known today because of the part it plays in the production of a Gloucestershire cheese, but other names tended to reflect their effects on drinkers: 'Merrylegs' and 'Mumblehead'! Most pears were unsuitable to eat but were more than suitable to turn into a superior perry.

Over time a lot of pear varieties have disappeared but luckily a few remain and so perry is still manufactured in the Forest today in places like Awre, where the Bull family has been brewing cider and perry for over three generations and in Blakeney, where James McCrindle brews traditionally.

James hand picks his fruit, presses it in small batches, and then ferments the perry in the bottle. He also produces a sparkling perry called 'Loiterpin', which earned him the title of British Champion Perry maker in 2014. This speciality perry is made by the methode champanoise, which uses champagne yeast and sugar and a twelve-month fermentation to produce a pleasing sparkling drink. James infers that there is evidence that the Forest was producing this brew in the 16th century and that the French purloined this idea.

The coming of the railway in the mid-19th century enabled mass producers of cider and perry to seek new markets, but it also allowed a new mass-produced beverage to infiltrate the Forest and thereby take over as the most popular drink in the area – BEER!

By 1841, beer was proving to be a popular drink, either sold in one of the 4 inns or 49 beerhouses in the Forest or even sold from front rooms of miners cottages who had paid the two guineas for a licence to do so. The early brews were called 'small beer' , low in alcohol and inexpensive. It was a grain-based drink, nicknamed 'liquid bread' that wasn't aged and thereby had no time to ferment. Those employed in heavy Forest industries, such as mining and quarrying, were known to slake their thirst with up to ten pints a day, which gave them much needed nutrition and calories. Even children and women drank the brew!

As its popularity grew so the art of beer making became more refined, and purpose-built breweries sprung up in the Forest, brewing stronger ales. The most famous Forest

Advertisement for Wintle's Brewery, Mitcheldean from 19th century

Workers outside the Burghams Redbrook Brewery in the late 19th century – Jenny Care Collection

brewery was Thomas Wintle's in Mitcheldean. Founded in 1868 it brewed with water from springs that were found in the nearby sandstone hills. It brewed mild, bitter and stout and the complex covered two acres of land. In 1926, it suffered a devastating fire and though it was repaired, Cheltenham Original Brewery bought it in 1930 and closed it seven years later. However today, in 2019, it houses the Bespoke Brewery, who sell handcrafted premium beers and cider throughout the Forest.

There were two breweries in Redbrook. Charles Herbert established the Old Redbrook Brewery in the 1840's and sold it to Thomas Burgham in 1856. Three generations of Burghams extended the business and eventually supplied at least 22 licensed premises, which were either owned or tied to the Redbrook Brewery. The wet grains were sold on to feed the swine in the Forest of Dean, transported there by pony and donkey. In 1923 Ind Coope and Co. took over the business and, in 1926, most of the brewery buildings were demolished.

A second brewery, further north, adjacent to Turnpike Gate House, near Redbrook Flour Mill at Upper Redbrook, was owned by James Hall and described as "house, offices, brewhouse, malt house and sheds". James ceased brewing in 1853 and became a wine and spirit merchant in Monmouth.

The Ruardean Brewery is known to have been around in 1891, owned by Evans and Robins, but in 1893 Edward Thompson bought the small affair and supplied local free houses. The business did not last long and was up for auction in 1912.

The Blakeney Brewery, also known as the Dean Forest Steam Brewery, was operated in the 1890s by Samuel Evans & Co., but was bought by Arnold Perrett of Wickwar in the early twentieth century.

The building of the railway and then the Severn Railway bridge saw breweries from across the river and further north in the county, take an interest in the Forest and gradually the local Forest breweries died out either permanently or amalgamated into the bigger distant concerns such as Stroud Brewery, Arnold Perret & Company of Wickwar and the Cheltenham Original Brewery.

The late twentieth century saw budding entrepreneurs try to revive the Forest brewing tradition in the form of microbreweries, but with varying success.

Hillside Brewery Porter

Hawthorn Brewery of Cinderford lasted only two years; the Freeminer Brewery lasted nine years, but Bespoke Brewery of Mitcheldean and Hillside Brewery near Longhope are proving very popular and successful.

Of course, not everyone from the nineteenth century wanted to drink alcohol, especially members of the Temperance movement! Some enterprising Forest businessmen decided to cash in on the stories about the recuperative ingredients in water that had made Bath, Cheltenham and Harrogate such meccas for pilgrims. The Forest had its own pilgrimage site – St Anthony's Well at Flaxley – where the waters could apparently cure skin complaints.

In Kelly's Directory of 1894 there is a John Ford, in the Forest, wine and spirit merchant, who also made Mineral Water. In 1899–1914, the Speech House Hotel housed George St John, who described himself as a mineral water and ginger beer manufacturer. The water came from a spring in the woods near the Hotel that was pumped through a pipe to the building.

There was, and still is, a lot of water in the Forest. The iron ore in the rocks meant the water was full of iron and therefore was a healthy drink, if not particularly appetising or safe.

Bottle of Speech House Mineral Water from the late 19th century –
Terry Halford

Other water companies sprung up (excuse the pun!), such as the Cinderford Aerated Water Company on the High Street, who produced "W.G" water, named after W G Grace, the Gloucestershire cricketer.

Bottle label for Lydbrook Valley Springs Company held at Dean Heritage Centre

There was also a Mineral Water Company in Lydney and Lydbrook had a spring water works from 1931, which produced various flavoured, aerated drinks and was locally called the 'Pop Factory'. The company had moved into a building that had housed a mineral water factory opened by G J Flewelling, a builder, just after WW1. The Lydbrook Valley Springs Company ceased trading in the late 1970s.

Bottle label for Lydbrook Valley Springs Company held at Dean Heritage Centre

H W Carter & Co advertisement from early 1950s.

After WW2 the Forest became famous for some soft drinks that were, and still are, produced in Coleford.

Ribena was a drink created by H W Carter & Company of Bristol between the wars. During WW2, it was part of the "Welfare Food" programme, which saw all blackberry production converted into syrup (or cordial) and given to children because of its high Vitamin C content. After the war the factory moved to Coleford, where it was marketed as a healthy drink to help fight tiredness and colds. Most of us still take a hot lemon and blackberry drink when a cold strikes! Today, in 2019, the company, now owned by Suntory, is still producing Ribena alongside 24 other soft drinks including the famous Lucozade.

Bottle of Lucozade from 1960s

Quosh Advertisement in 1955 from
Coleford: A Social History

Lucozade is a drink associated with illness, so perhaps not an ideal accompaniment to our menu, though today it has been rebranded as a sports energy drink.

In the 1950s the factory developed 'Quosh', a fruit squash that came in various flavours, such as orange, lemon, lime and grapefruit and some mixed with barley. Unfortunately, it is no longer produced in the Forest, but would have been an acceptable drink to have with this feast.

To finish this section of the menu I do have a couple of recipes for homemade drinks that were very popular in the Forest, made from foraged ingredients, which can be found today.

The elder tree (or Ellum, as it is known in the Forest) produces beautiful white flowers in the spring. If left on the tree they develop into purple berries. Many Foresters

Elder blossom and berries – thereisagreen.me

would pick the flowers and either use them fresh immediately to make cordials or teas, or dry for use later. The berries would be picked later on in the year to turn into a syrup to use during the winter for refreshment or in medicines. A special drink was often made from the blossom and I think it is a fitting drink to wash down any choices from this menu.

FOREST ELLUM BLO' CHAMPAGNE

1¼ lbs sugar	1 gallon boiling water
6-8 elderflower heads (picked on a sunny day)	1 lemon – finely sliced
2 tbsps white wine vinegar	

Add the sugar to the boiling water and stir until dissolved. Leave it to go cold. Add the elderflower heads plus the lemon and vinegar. Leave to stand for 24 hours. Strain and decant in screw top bottles. It will be ready in 1-2 weeks and will provide a light fizzy drink for children. Left longer it will become a slightly alcoholic drink for adults. Store in a dry, cool place.

Dried elderflower heads can be used later to make the drink but may need more sugar to obtain the fizziness!

In Celtic mythology, the hawthorn tree symbolised love and protection. It was also known as the Fairy tree, with fairies living under the branches, acting as the trees

Hawthorn berries – verywellhealth.com

guardians. Its abundant fruits provided Foresters with the ingredients to make a wine, which was used for refreshment as well as like the elder, for medicinal purposes. The berries contain properties that are a benefit to the cardiovascular system.

The most difficult part about making HAWTHORN WINE is picking the berries. Watch out for the thorns and make sure you have anti-septic cream handy for your scratches!

First pick over and wash the berries. For every quart of berries (1 quart = about 1 lb) add an equal quantity of cold water. To every gallon, allow two lemons (sliced and including the pips). After soaking the berries for 10 days, strain and add to every gallon of liquid 3 lbs of sugar and ½ oz of yeast. The yeast should have previously been soaked in ½ pint of lukewarm liquid. Cover the wine with a cloth and place in a warm area. Once it froths, pop into jars or barrels. Bottle only when the May flower is in bloom (late April, early May) to ensure a clear, sparkling wine.

At the beginning of this book, I wrote about the influence of the Romans on some of the foodstuffs available to Foresters. It is common knowledge that Romans enjoyed the odd glass of WINE, but there is no evidence that they actually grew grapes or made wine while in occupation. However, it seems quite possible that by the time of the Norman Conquest there were vineyards in the country, a substantial number owned by monasteries, found mainly in southern England. The wine they produced was not for general consumption, so if wine was produced at Tintern or Flaxley, it is unlikely the common labourer would not have had access to it. We know that Foresters did make their own drinks, loosely called wines, from fruits and flowers they found or grew, but there is no record of vines growing in workers gardens. By the time of Henry VIII, there were 139 vineyards in Southern England and Wales, but after the Reformation, there was a steep decline, probably because of the dissolution of the monasteries who owned the crops.

In the 20th century there is some evidence that grape juice was imported from France but not to make wine – it was mixed with cider to produce some very potent drinks! Today, in the 21st century, there are four successful vineyards close to the Forest, producing good quality wine that rivals anything from abroad. Ancre Hill at Monmouth, Parva Farm at Tintern and Three Choirs and Strawberry Hill at Newent are award-winning vineyards, producing good quality still and sparkling wines and in Longhope, there is another wine producer that keeps the true heritage of Forest wine production going. VQ Country Wines is based on a farm, where they grow their own fruit, vegetables and flowers that end up in a wide selection of wines. All wines are seasonal, the produce is handpicked, and then the wine is made in small batches. There is a choice of Crab Apple, Marrow, Medlar, Oak Leaf, Birch Sap, Blaisdon Plum and Pear to name just a few.

So Cheers!

BILL PLEASE, WAITER!

So there we are – some of the Forest of Dean's Food and Drink heritage.

I have only covered a small part of what Foresters ate and drank in days gone by, but I hope you will have gained an idea of what tantalised Foresters taste buds.

There were simple local dishes that I have not mentioned, such as SCOW DOUGH, a bread dough that was cooked with ham inside and then there are recipes such as LAMB'S TAIL PIE and MUGGETY PIE (made from the umbilical cords of calves). I have even left off the menu POOR MAN'S GOOSE (no goose was harmed in the preparation of this dish!) and SHEEP'S HEAD STEW. CHITTLINGS have also been ignored, as has BAKED HEDGEHOG. Then there are the desserts such as THIMBLE MILL PUDDING, a suet-based apple sweet, or FOREST PUDDING, a little like a Spotted Dick. Then there is FOREST JELLY made with ground rice, sago and pearl barley and then sweetened with fruit. In addition, I must not forget GINGERBREAD HUSBANDS or SHY CAKE to accompany your cup of tea or even MANGOLD WINE or POTATO WINE.

I could go on, but I won't.

Thank you for reading – BON APPETIT.

CONVERSION TABLES

Temperature Conversions

Fahrenheit	Celsius	Gas Mark	Description
225	107	¼	Very Low
250	121	½	Very Low
275	135	1	Low
300	149	2	Low
325	163	3	Moderate
350	177	4	Moderate
375	190	5	Moderately Hot
400	204	6	Moderately Hot
425	218	7	Hot
450	238	8	Hot
475	246	9	Very Hot

Liquid Capacity Conversion

Imperial	Metric
1 tablespoon	15 ml
2 tablespoons	30 ml
4 tablespoons	60 ml
¼ pint	150 ml
⅓ pint	200 ml
½ pint	300 ml
¾ pint	450 ml
1 pint	600 ml
1 ½ pint	900 ml
2 pint	1.25 litres
4 pint	2.5 litres
8 pint/I gallon	5 litres

Weight Conversions

Imperial	Metric
½ oz	14 g
1 oz	28 g
2 oz	57 g
3 oz	85 g
4 oz	113 g
5 oz	142 g
6 oz	170 g
7 oz .	199 g
8 oz	227 g
9 oz	255 g
10 oz	284 g
12 oz	340 g
1 lb	454 g
1 ½ lb	680 g
2 lb	907 g
2.2 lb	1 kg

ACKNOWLEDGEMENTS

Websites

Glamorousglutton.com

Books.google.co.uk

Mytask.uk

Oakden.co.uk

Picturesofengland.com

Theransomnote.com

Britannia.com

Informationforbritain.co.uk

Greenchronicle.com

Contributors

The Speech House Hotel

Smarts Cheesery

Harts Barn Cookery School

Bream Gardening Society

Dean Heritage Centre

Gloucester Records Office

John Metherall & The Dean Forest Railway Museum

TV

BBC2 Inside The Factory 16th January 2018

Books

A Glance Back at Lydbrook by Lydbrook Historical Society – Black Dwarf Publications 2002

A Glance Back at Mitcheldean by Paul Mason – Black Dwarf Publication 2001

A Glance Back at Coleford by K & J Webb – Black Dwarf Publications 2000

Aspects of Awre by Awre Millennium Committee – Black Dwarf Publication 2001

Dean Forest Kitchen (in aid of NSPCC) – Douglas Maclean 1979

The Platelayers Trolley by Dean Forest Railway 1979

100 Gloucestershire Recipes Old & New by Gloucestershire Federation of WIs – Countryside Publications Ltd 1979

Traditional Gloucestershire Recipes by Jo and Merlin Price – Minimax Books 1985

A Taste of Gloucestershire & The Cotswolds by Julie Skinner – Francis Frith Collection 2012

Gleanings from Gloucestershire Housewives – WI Federation 1936

The Pubs of the Royal Forest of Dean by Heather Hurley – Logaston Press 2004

A Drink in the Forest by Steve Pritchard & John Saunders – Steve Pritchard 2010

The River Hobbler's Apprentice by Alan Butt – The History Press Ltd 2009

Fish Food from the Waters by Harlan Walker – Prospect Books 1998

Forest Voices by Humphrey Phelps – Amberley Publishing 2008

Where I Belong by Joyce Latham – Alan Sutton Publishing 1993

Full Hearts and Empty Bellies by Winifred Foley – Abacus 2009

Collected Poems 1912-1957 by F W Harvey – Douglas Maclean 1983

Coleford: A Social Guide by The Community Association 1955

Inside

Other books by this author:

The tiny hamlet of Whitecroft in the Forest of Dean is known as Dabdown to its locals, who are nicknamed 'The Greeks'. It has no shops or school or church but two real ale pubs! But it has a claim to fame: it was the original home of a factory that produced "Marigold Gloves". It was this nugget of information that sowed the seed for the author's research into the history of the village.

Over 1400 people a day used to visit to work, shop or play. Industry thrived and champion rugby, football and cricket teams won accolades. A highly regarded Male Voice Choir provided entertainment and shops provided retail therapy selling everything from buttons to batteries and meat to millinery. At one time, there were four sweet shops rotting the village children's teeth!

Meet the people of 'Dabdown' and discover how this once thriving hive of activity has changed over nearly 200 years.

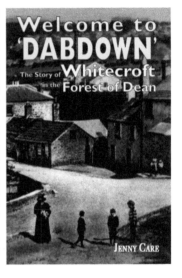

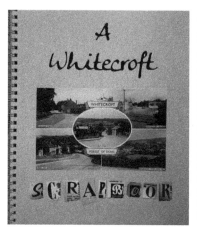

A Whitecroft Scrapbook

ISBN : 9780995595255

This is a book full of photographs and articles from the late 19th century up to present day. The images have been donated by villagers and former inhabitants of this small hamlet that once had sixteen shops, four large employers including a world famous pin factory and the home of 'Marigold' kitchen gloves. They are all closed now. There was also a thriving Wesleyan Chapel and three pubs that all helped to install a marvellous community spirit. Funds raised from this book will go towards the Memorial Hall Defibrillator Fund.